CONTENTS

KU-477-801

FRANCE: PAST AND PRESENT

French history

France is the largest country in Western Europe with the fourth largest number of people. It shares its border with six other countries, from Spain in the south-west to Belgium in the north-east.

France was conquered by Julius Caesar in 52BC. At that time, it was known as Gaul. The area remained part of the **Roman Empire** for 500 years. Between 1152 and 1453, large parts of France were ruled by England.

France grew rich under its own kings, but the wars in which it became involved were costly. Rich and poor people became discontented with the high **taxes** they had to pay. In 1789, the French Revolution took place. As a result, King Louis XVI was executed and France became a **republic**.

In the early 1800s, France, led by the emperor Napoleon, attacked other countries in Europe, the Far East and Russia. All these lands were lost again when the French army was defeated at the Battle of Waterloo in 1815. Now France has a president as head of state instead of a king or emperor.

The Eiffel Tower in Paris.
- *The 300-metre high tower was built in 1889.*
- *The man who designed it was named Gustave Eiffel.*
- *The tower was built as part of an international exhibition held in Paris.*
- *The tallest building in London is the Canary Wharf office tower at 244 metres.*

France

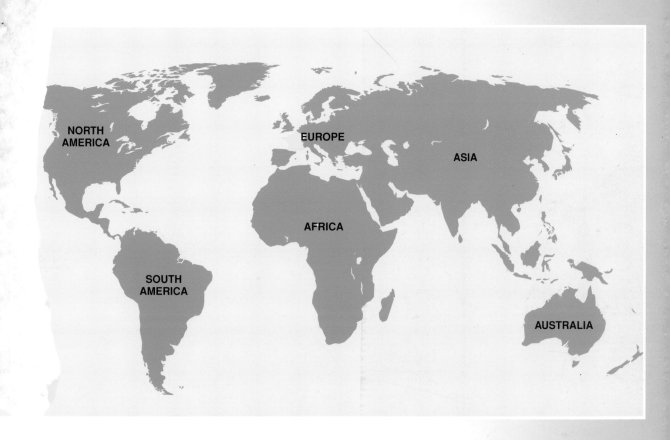

NORTH AMERICA

EUROPE

ASIA

AFRICA

SOUTH AMERICA

AUSTRALIA

Fred Martin

Heinemann

First published in Great Britain by Heinemann Library
Halley Court, Jordan Hill, Oxford OX2 8EJ
a division of Reed Educational and Professional Publishing Ltd

OXFORD FLORENCE PRAGUE MADRID ATHENS
MELBOURNE AUCKLAND KUALA LUMPUR SINGAPORE TOKYO
IBADAN NAIROBI KAMPALA JOHANNESBURG GABORONE
PORTSMOUTH NH CHICAGO MEXICO CITY SAO PAULO

Designed by AMR
Illustrations by Art Construction
Printed in Hong Kong by Wing King Tong Co. Ltd.

02 01 00 99
10 9 8 7 6 5 4 3 2

ISBN 0 431 01353 5
This title is also available in a hardback library edition (ISBN 0 431 01352 7).

British Library Cataloguing in Publication Data
Martin, Fred, 1948-
Next Stop France
1. France – Geography – Juvenile literature
I.Title II.France
914.4

Acknowledgements
The Publishers would like to thank the following for permission to reproduce photographs:
ALLSPORT P. Rondeau p.26; Bridgeman Art Library/Giraudon p.29; Colorific! D. Berretty p.18, Boccon-Gibod/Black Star p.23, Carl Purcell p.7; J. Allen Cash Ltd pp.8, 24; Trevor Clifford pp.4, 12-13, 16-17, 19, 21, 25, 26; Robert Harding Picture Library Vandermarst p.14; Trip A. M. Bazalik p.6, C. Bland p.22, D. Brooker p.5, B. Hills p.9, W. Newlands p.20, D. Ray p.28, D. Saunders p.27, A. Tovy pp.10-11; ZEFA p.15.

Cover photograph reproduced with permission of Tony Stone Images, Michael Brusselle.

Our thanks to Sèverine Jeauneau for her comments in the preparation of this book.

Every effort has been made to contact holders of any material reproduced in this book. Any omissions will be rectified in subsequent printings if notice is given to the Publisher.

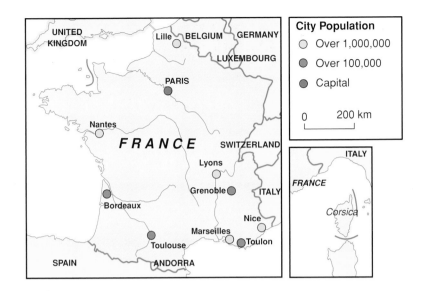

City Population
- ○ Over 1,000,000
- ● Over 100,000
- ● Capital

0   200 km

FRANCE / ITALY / Corsica

Modern France

There was an enormous amount of damage done to France during both World Wars, when it was occupied by Germany. But France has recovered and built a modern economy from the wartime ruins.

The **population** of France is now about 58 million. Most people in France are proud that they are part of one nation. This means that they feel they are part of the same country, have the same language and work together for the good of their country.

In recent years people have moved to France from other parts of the world. Most have come from places that were once ruled by France, such as Senegal and Algeria in Africa. These are countries where many people still speak French.

France is one of the least crowded countries in Europe. On average, there are 105 people in every square kilometre, compared to 234 in the UK. However, some places, such as Paris, are very densely populated.

A typical château [sha-toh] in the countryside in the south-west of France.
- *Grapes are growing in the château's vineyard.*
- *This sort of countryside attracts many tourists to France.*

5

THE NATURAL LANDSCAPE

The Ardèche gorge in the southern district of Provence.
- *The winding river has cut down through the limestone uplands.*

Lowland France

There are large areas of lowland in France called basins. The rock in these lowland areas is often soft clay. Harder rocks, such as chalk and limestone, form ridges that rise above the lowlands. In the north there is the Paris basin. In the south-west, the Aquitaine basin extends from the Atlantic coast to the Massif Central highlands.

Most people live in these lowland areas. One reason for this is that it is much easier to build houses, factories and offices where land is flat. Farming is also easier in lowland areas.

Wide rivers and their smaller **tributary** rivers flow through the lowland basins. The rivers Seine [sen] and Loire [lwar] flow through the Paris basin. The River Garonne flows through the Aquitaine basin. Roads and railway lines have been built along these valleys making it easier to get from place to place.

Mountain landscapes

The highest mountain ranges in France are the Alps in the south-east and the Pyrenees in the south-west. These mountains were pushed up from an ancient sea-bed about 30 million years ago. Now they have steep slopes, high mountain peaks and deep valleys with fast-flowing rivers. There is always snow and ice near the mountain peaks. Rivers of ice called **glaciers** slowly move down some of the highest valleys.

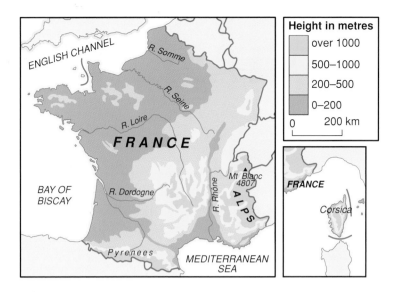

The Vosges [vauj] and Jura mountains in the east are lower and less steep. In the north-west, France's oldest rocks form a giant **peninsula** of high land called the Brittany peninsula.

The Massif plateau

The Massif Central is a **plateau** where the surface of the land is high but mainly flat. In some places there are deep gorges with rivers flowing through them, such as the Lot and Tarn. There are also the remains of old volcanoes. There are lakes where the craters used to be.

The strangest features in this area are steep, pointed hills called **puys** [pwee]. These are made from sticky **lava** that moved towards the Earth's surface then cooled down. The weather has not yet been able to wear them away completely.

The highest peak in France is *Mont Blanc* in the Alps. It reaches a height of 4807 metres. *Mont Blanc* is on the border with Italy, where it is called *Monte Bianco*.

The Canal de Bourgone is linked to the River Seine in the north of France.
- *The landscape in this area is mainly flat with some steep slopes called escarpments.*
- *The escarpments rise to form low hills.*

CLIMATE, VEGETATION AND WILDLIFE

Playing boules *in Port Grimaud in the south of France.*

- *The south of France often has hot and dry summer weather.*
- *Too much sun can cause sunburn and other health problems.*
- *Boules is often played in the evening after work and when it is cooler outside.*

Climates in France

If you travelled through France, you would get a feel for its varied climate. You could go from Brittany's mild and damp weather in the north-west, through the varied temperatures of inland Alsace, to the hot, dry summers of the Mediterranean coast in the south.

Temperature, wind and rain

Mild and wet air blows over France from the Atlantic Ocean in the west. This helps keep the temperature mild in winter. In summer, these ocean winds help keep the air temperature down.

In the east, it is a little warmer in summer, but very cold air sometimes blows across the continent of Europe during winter. This air starts its journey over the frozen ice and snow of central Russia. It is still bitterly cold by the time it reaches Paris.

The hottest temperatures are usually found in the south. In summer, the sun is much higher in the sky than over places further north. There is usually very little rain during the summer months. If it does rain, it can be very heavy with thunder, lightning and hail.

Winter weather in the south can be very wet. This happens when wet air from the Atlantic Ocean moves across the land and drops its water as rain. Sometimes there is flooding when too much rain falls quickly in a short time. Rainwater flows into the rivers and they quickly overflow their banks.

The vegetation

There are not many places left in France where natural vegetation can still be seen. The oak and other **deciduous** woodlands of the north have been cut down to make space for farming. In the south, the drier scrubland and pines have been cleared for the same reason. Although about a quarter of France is forested, much of this has been recently planted to grow trees for timber.

The Mistral is the name given to an unusual cold and strong wind that sometimes blows south over the Mediterranean lowlands. The cold air blows down the Rhône [rown] valley. The wind blows at speeds of up to 100 kilometres per hour. The Mistral is able to blow down crops and make life very unpleasant.

The Camargue is a marshland area on the Mediterranean coast of France.
- *Wildlife, such as wading birds and some wild horses, live in this area.*
- *Some parts of the Camargue have been drained and used for farming and building.*

9

TOWNS AND CITIES

A history of towns and cities

Three out of every four people in France live in a town or city. Some were started by the Romans about 2000 years ago. Others grew in the Middle Ages or from about 200 years ago during the Industrial Revolution. The size of most towns and cities is still growing as new houses, shops and factories are built.

Types of towns

There are **industrial towns** where people work in factories making goods such as cars. In some towns, there is a history of making one type of product such as cloth in Lille or aircraft in Toulouse. There are also towns where tourists come to visit. The historic towns of Dinan and Carcassonne are two of the most popular. Nice is one of the main seaside resorts.

Some towns are where there is a meeting place for roads, railways, shipping and aircraft routes. The sea port of Marseilles [mar-say] on the Mediterranean coast is one of these. Smaller ports such as Dieppe are important as cross-channel ferry ports.

A view of Paris from the Eiffel Tower.
- *The River Seine flows through the centre of Paris.*
- *The central part of the city is densely packed with flats, shops, offices, places of entertainment and government buildings.*

There are the hundreds of small market towns scattered over France. These are places where farmers sell their produce and buy what they need. All except the smallest towns have a mayor and a town hall called the *Hôtel de Ville*.

Paris the capital

Paris is the largest city and the country's **capital city**. The city sprawls out over the Seine valley and the Paris basin lowlands. The River Seine divides the city almost in half. There are offices, factories, shops and every other type of business in Paris, just like in most other cities around the world. There are also theatres, restaurants and street cafés where people can enjoy themselves.

Many Parisians live in flats in old buildings near the city centre. Others live in houses and blocks of modern flats in the **suburbs** near the countryside. Some completely new towns have been built in the countryside outside Paris, to stop it becoming too big.

Paris began at a place where the River Seine could be crossed by using an island as a stepping stone. A tribe named the Parisii lived on the island. The island is now called the Ile de la Cité. Paris became the capital city of a tribe called the Franks in AD506. France is named after the Franks.

Cannes [can] is on France's Mediterranean coast.
- *It is a centre for the tourist industry.*
- *An international film festival is held at Cannes every year.*

THE PARISIANS

The rue du Printemps

The Dupleix [dewpleh] family live in the rue du Printemps (Spring Street), in the central part of Paris. It is only a few minutes' walk to famous sights such as the Champs Elysées [shonz-eleezeh] and the Arc de Triomphe.

They live in an apartment in a building that was built just over one hundred years ago. It is a very densely built-up part of Paris, where people cannot have a garden. But it is a lively part of the city, where there are plenty of shops and places for entertainment. There are many street cafés in the district, both for local people and for the tourists who come to see the sights.

Le petit déjeuner (breakfast).
- *This is a simple quick meal with coffee, bread and jam.*
- *The family home is neat and bright with furniture to suit the age of the house.*

Claire Dupleix does most of her shopping in the local small shops and the street market.

Work and school

Tanguy Dupleix is aged 42 and his wife, Claire, is aged 41. Tanguy is an architect. His wife has a part-time job as a secretary with the same firm. Tanguy goes to work on a motorbike. Traffic in the central part of Paris is always very heavy, so it is quicker to travel by motorbike. It is also hard to find anywhere to park a car. Tanguy works very long hours, often from 7.00 am until 8.00 pm, or even later.

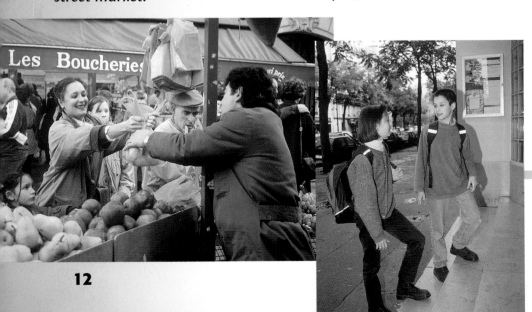

The two eldest children walk to school.

The family sometimes play board games such as Scrabble.

There are four children in the family. The two girls are Camille who is 13, and Clotilde who is seven. The boys are Leonard, aged 11 and Louis, aged five. All the children are now old enough to go to school. The older children walk there. It takes them only ten minutes.

Camille is learning to play the flute and Leonard is learning the piano.

Family life

The family enjoy a good standard of living. They employ a cleaner to help do the housework. Like most French families, they enjoy good food. Breakfast is usually a simple meal of coffee, bread and jam. Two of their favourite dinners are local dishes called *Boeuf Mode* and *Blanquette de veau*. Claire Dupleix does most of the shopping in small local shops and the street markets. She knows how to pick the best vegetables, fruit, cheeses and other food from the counters.

The family sometimes play board games at home. These include games such as *Scrabble*, *Monopoly* and *Pictionary*. Camille is learning to play the flute. Sometimes her brother Leonard accompanies her by playing the piano. Tanguy likes to go running, though this is not easy through the streets of Paris. There is a half-marathon through Paris every year. Thousands of people enter the race, though Tanguy is not one of them.

Tanguy Dupleix goes to work on his motorbike

FARMING LANDSCAPES

A farming landscape in Lectour, south-west France.
• The gentle slopes and warm climate make this area suitable for different types of **arable** farming.

Farming districts

France is known the world over for its food, especially its cheeses and its fine wines. Types of wine and cheese often take their name from the area where they are produced. Champagne comes from the Champagne district to the north-east of Paris and brie cheese originated in Brie to the south of Paris.

The farming landscape looks very different from place to place. There are large farms and fields in the lowlands such as in the Paris **basin**. Crops such as wheat are grown in this area. In other places, such as in Brittany, farms are much smaller. Cows graze in small fields surrounded by hedgerows.

Types of farming

The type of farming in each area is affected by the climate. Brittany in the north-west has a wet but mild climate. Grass for cattle grows well here. There is less rain further south and east. This area is better for crops such as maize (corn) and sunflowers.

The slopes and height of the land also affect what is farmed there. It is easy to farm crops using **combine harvesters** on the gentle slopes of the Paris basin. Slopes are much steeper in upland areas such as the Massif Central. This makes it harder to use machinery so cattle and sheep are reared instead.

Crops such as wheat grow best where the soil is deep, fertile and does not become too wet. Grass grows best when there is more rain and where there is more water in the soil.

French vineyards

Wine is made from the juice of grapes that grow on **vines**. A field of vines is called a vineyard. Whole hillsides in wine-growing regions such as the Rhône Valley are covered with vineyards. Vines grow best in the warm and dry parts of France. Slopes that face the south are often used for vines because they get more sun.

Picking grapes in south-west France.
- *The area south of Bordeaux is one of the main areas for growing grapes and making wine in France.*

France is the world's second largest producer of wine, the second largest producer of sugar beet, the fifth largest producer of milk and is eighth in the world for producing cereals such as wheat.

THE COUNTRY LIFE

The French château

The Jussiaux [jewsyo] family live in a house in the grounds of a French château. The château is an old stately home. It is now owned by the local town of Falaise, in Normandy. This is the region that is nearest to England across the English Channel. Falaise is about 50 km inland from the city and ferry port of Caen. The château is open to the public for visits, as well as being run as a riding school.

The Jussiaux family and their dogs outside their home.

A riding school

Isabelle Jussiaux is in charge of the riding school. She teaches children to ride. There are 40 horses at the riding school. Most of them are New Forest Ponies. At the weekend, Isabelle goes to horse-riding and show-jumping shows. Her eldest daughter, Camille, sometimes enters pony club competitions. Isabelle used to live in Paris, but now enjoys a very different kind of life-style in the country.

Isabelle's husband, Dominique, also works with the horses. His job is to breed them and to break them in, so they are suitable for the riding school.

The evening meal of pasta with a rabbit stew.
- *There is a selection of French cheeses on the table.*
- *Thomas wants to play with his toy animals.*

Home life

The first job every morning is to feed the horses. Then the family have breakfast of coffee, with bread and jam or chocolate spread. Dominique and Isabelle have two children. Camille is aged seven and Thomas her brother is aged four. After breakfast, Isabelle drives the children to school. Camille goes to a primary school, while Thomas attends a nursery school. The main meal is usually in the evening when all the family are together.

Falaise is a country town where there is a good range of small shops and a market. There is a supermarket outside the town that the family sometimes visits. There are many local, Normandy foods, such as the cheese called *camembert*.

The family are happy to live at the château in this part of France. It is an attractive part of the country with a very different lifestyle from that of the busy cities.

Dominique's job is to feed and look after the horses.

Some of the stables in the grounds of the château.

WHAT'S IN FRENCH SHOPS?

Hypermarkets

The first **hypermarket** in Europe was opened in France near Paris in 1963. A hypermarket is a giant shop that sells almost everything a shopper might want to buy. Food, drink, clothes, toys, garden equipment and electrical goods can all be bought under one roof.

Hypermarkets are usually built on the edge of big towns and cities. They are usually on one floor so that people can use a trolley to buy goods in bulk. They have car parks that can take several thousands of cars and where people can park for free.

Carrefour, Leclerc and *Intermarché* are three of the biggest companies who run hypermarkets. About 90,000 people work in the *Carrefour* hypermarkets throughout France.

People from the UK sometimes cross the English Channel to do their shopping in hypermarkets in Boulogne and near Calais. The price of some goods, such as alcoholic drinks, is cheaper in France. The quality and choice of goods such as clothes also attracts people from the UK.

Shopping inside a supermarket.
- *Supermarkets and the larger hypermarkets offer shoppers an enormous choice of good quality food at the lowest prices.*
- *Shoppers fill trolleys with goods they can buy in bulk.*

Small specialist shops

As well as the hypermarkets and supermarkets, France still has many small specialist shops. The *boulangerie* makes and sells bread and cakes to local people who prefer to eat them freshly baked. Small shops called *le bar tabac* sell cigarettes, drinks and postage stamps.

There are different shops for selling different types of meat. A *boucherie* sells cuts of uncooked meat while the *charcuterie* sells **processed** meats such as pies, pâté and sausages. The *poissonerie* [pwa-sonery] is where fish are sold.

Market stalls

Most villages and towns have a weekly open-air market. Farmers and traders set up their stalls in the market square. Sometimes a whole street is closed to traffic for the weekly market. Fresh vegetables, fish and meats are sold. French shoppers are skilled at picking the best produce from what is on sale.

Sadly, these traditional markets are disappearing as more people move over to shopping in hypermarkets for convenience.

The Cité Europe is a new shopping complex near Calais at the entrance to the Channel Tunnel. It covers several floors and has all the shops and restaurants of a small town, but in one building. Many people from the UK now visit the Cité Europe to do their shopping. The journey through the Channel Tunnel takes less than 30 minutes.

FOOD AND COOKING

A love of food

A *cordon bleu* chef is one who has reached the highest standards. It is not surprising that the award comes from the French. For them food and cooking are taken seriously and are talked about as much as the weather is in the UK.

Bread is a basic food that is eaten with most meals. This is usually a long crusty roll of bread called a *baguette*. This has to be eaten on the day it is bought as it goes stale quickly. For breakfast, a croissant, or a *pain au chocolat* (a croissant with chocolate inside) is sometimes eaten.

Main meals can have several courses accompanied by wine. As an *hors d'oeuvre* [or-dervre], the first course, there might be soup or some fresh mixed vegetables. The main meat or fish course is then served. This is followed by cheese and fresh fruit, or sometimes by dessert. Wine is chosen to suit each course.

Eating out in a restaurant.
- *The food is always perfectly prepared, well presented and comes in several courses.*
- *Glasses of wine and water go with the meal.*

Buying meat in a small local shop in Paris.

Cooking styles

There are two main styles of cooking. One is called *haute cuisine*. This is the high-class cooking mainly done in the most expensive restaurants. Most cooking done in the home is simpler.

Each region has its own special types of food made with local produce. Quiche Lorraine is a pastry dish with a filling of chopped bacon, cream and eggs. This comes from the Lorraine region in eastern France. In the coastal regions of Brittany and Normandy, there are fish dishes made with freshly caught mussels, oysters and small shrimps called *crevettes*. Lobster cooked in a cream sauce is called *homard à l'armoricaine*.

Meat specialities

Meat such as steak, lamb, horse and veal from young calves are all cooked in a variety of ways, often with a strongly flavoured sauce. *Coq au vin* is a dish of chicken cooked in red wine. Garlic is used to give more flavour to many dishes.

Some types of snail, or *escargots*, are eaten cooked in a garlic, butter and parsley sauce. Pâté is made from chopped pieces of different types of meat. *Foie gras* [fwah-grah], a meat delicacy, is made by overfeeding geese to make their livers grow bigger. The liver is then eaten like a pâté.

Truffles are special wild mushrooms that grow both above and under the ground in woodland areas. Pigs or dogs are used to sniff them out. Once found, the location of truffles is a closely guarded secret as they are hard to find and expensive to buy.

MADE IN FRANCE

Making wealth

France is one of the world's largest producers of goods made in factories. Selling these goods both in France and **exporting** them to other countries is what helps make the country rich.

The first large factories in France were usually in places where there was coal in the ground. This is because coal was used to power machinery but it was expensive to transport it very far. The towns in Nord-Pas-de-Calais such as Lille and Lens grew for this reason. Rocks such as iron ore were dug out of the ground and melted to make iron and steel.

Some coal is still mined in France and there are still some iron and steel factories, but the old industries are no longer as important as they once were.

Fashions and food products

Paris is known as an international centre for the fashion industry. Buyers from all over the world come to see the latest fashions paraded on the catwalks. Many of these clothes are made in Paris and in other towns and cities both in France and in other countries.

A factory which processes uranium ore.
- *Uranium is the fuel used in nuclear power stations.*
- *About 70% of all electricity in France is generated in nuclear power stations.*

Much of the produce from farms goes to factories where it is **processed** and put into bottles, packets or tins. Milk is processed to make butter and cheese. Grapes are made into wine and sunflower seeds are crushed to produce oil.

Leading in technology

Cars made in France are sold all over Europe and in many other countries. Renault and Peugeot-Citröen are two of the most well-known makes. Michelin car tyres have been made in Clermont Ferrand since 1876.

In 1909, a Frenchman named Louis Blériot became the first man to fly across the English Channel. This was in a plane he built himself. Now giant Airbus passenger aircraft are made in Toulouse. Parts for these aircraft are also made in the UK and flown to Toulouse. A special aircraft has had to be built to fly larger pieces, such as wings, between the UK and France.

Building an Airbus airliner in Toulouse.
- *France, the UK and other countries work together to build both passenger and military aircraft.*

In the future, the production of many more goods in France will depend on using **advanced technology** such as computers and robots. In this way goods can be made at the highest quality for the lowest cost. Industrial estates with high-technology industries are being set up all over France. This should mean that France continues to be one of the world's richest **manufacturing** countries.

About 3.5 million cars are made in France every year. This makes it fourth in the world behind Japan, the USA and Germany.

TRANSPORT AND TRAVEL

High-speed travel

The old main roads in France are called the **Routes Nationales**. They are often very straight and lined with trees. The speed limit outside towns is 90 kilometres per hour or 110 kilometres per hour on the larger dual carriageway roads.

The **Autoroutes** are long-distance motorways such as the one from Paris to Marseilles on the Mediterranean coast. Motorists have to pay a **toll** to use these roads. The usual speed limit is 130 kilometres per hour.

In 1981, the 'train à grande vitesse', or TGV, began a route between Paris and Lyon. This is one of the world's fastest trains with a top speed of about 300 kilometres per hour. Now there are regular TGV services to other major cities and more are still being built.

The Channel Tunnel between Folkestone in the UK and Coquelles near Calais in France was opened in 1994. The tunnel is for trains only. It is 50 kilometres long, with almost 38 kilometres running under the sea.

TGV high-speed trains at the Monparnasse station in Paris.
- *The trains in the photo are used on the TGV Atlantique route between Paris and Bordeaux.*
- *The train takes about three hours to travel 550 kilometres.*

Traffic in Paris on the Champs Elysées.
- *Eight out of every ten households have at least one car.*
- *Ring roads have been built on the outskirts and in the centre of Paris, but traffic is still a major problem.*

Flying times

About 12 million people fly between the main cities on regular **domestic flights**. An air fare is usually more expensive than a train fare, but the travel time is about three times faster.

Paris has two airports – Roissy-Charles de Gaulle and Orly. Another, named Santeuil, is to be built near Chartres. Roissy-Charles de Gaulle is mainly for **international flights**.

Inland waterways

The rivers Seine and Rhône are the two most used inland **waterways**. Canals link some of the main rivers, especially in the north where there is more industry and therefore more heavy **freight** to move. There are just over 8000 kilometres of inland waterways.

Most rivers are unsuitable for barges. They are either too shallow, flow too quickly or the amount of water in them changes too much during the year. Some rivers, such as the Seine, have been made **navigable** by dredging, building locks and weirs to control the river's speed, and by building reservoirs to keep up the flow of water all year.

In April 1996, the *Navire à Grande Vitesse* began a regular service between Nice and the French island of Corsica. This high-speed ship can carry 500 passengers and travel at 40 knots. The journey takes only three hours – half the previous time for a ferry to travel to Corsica.

LEISURE AND SPORT

Looking good, keeping fit

Most people in France like to look good and keep fit. About three-quarters of all males and about half of all females regularly take part in a sport. The most popular sports are football, rugby, cycling, tennis, skiing and golf.

The *Tour de France* is a cycle race that takes the cyclists on a 2300-kilometre tour around the country. The winner of each part of the race wears a yellow jersey during the next stage. The race usually lasts about 23 days and finishes in Paris.

The *Le Mans* 24-hour motor car race and the Monaco Grand Prix are also big sporting events that attract thousands of spectators.

Skiing is popular in mountain areas such as the Alps, the Pyrenees and the Massif Central. Chamonix [shamoh-nee] in the French Alps is one of the main centres for skiing.

The **Tour de France** *is one of France's most popular sporting events.*
- *The race leader wears the yellow jersey.*

A mountain ski resort in Val d'Isère in the French Alps.
- Skiing is a very popular family sport.
- Children are often put on skis almost as soon as they can walk!

Local leisure

There are places in every French town and village where people meet in the evenings to play *boules.* The aim is to throw a metal ball at a small ball, to see who comes closest or even hits the small ball. Because the ground is usually uneven, the best way to do this is to throw the ball high into the air.

Although almost every family has a television set, visiting the cinema is still a popular way to spend an evening. There are 4400 cinemas in France. Many of the films have been made in France though some are brought in from the USA and the UK.

Seaside and Disney

France has a 5500-kilometre coastline and holidays are often spent camping near the coast, especially in the south of France along the Mediterranean Sea. Motorways to the south are always jammed at the start of the summer holiday in August. There are also good beaches along the Bay of Biscay and in the sandy coves of Brittany.

One of the newest places for entertainment is Euro Disneyland on the edge of Paris. This is a giant **theme park** with adventure rides and other types of entertainment as well as hotels, restaurants and a campsite. People can visit Disneyland Paris for a day, or stay there for a week.

Disneyland Paris is 1943 hectares in size. This is about one-fifth of the total size of Paris!

CUSTOMS AND ARTS

National festivals and customs

Bastille [bas-tee] Day on 14 July is a day for celebration in France. This was the day in 1789 when people in Paris attacked the Bastille prison. This is often seen as the start of the French Revolution. French people feel that the revolution made them free from the king and **aristocracy** who had controlled their lives.

On 1 May each year, French people give each other little bunches of lily-of-the-valley. This is done as a sign of friendship.

Festivals old and new

There are local festivals at different times of the year all over France. Some are religious. Others are to do with local farming and fishing. One of these is on St John's Day in Brittany. People from the fishing villages dress in traditional costumes and walk through the towns and villages. Bands play traditional music and folk groups perform dances.

There are also some modern festivals, such as the Cannes film festival. This is where awards are given for the best performers and directors in film and music. Famous actors and actresses from all over the world go to Cannes to receive prizes or just to be seen.

The Mardi gras *festival in Nice on the Mediterranean coast.*
- *The name* Mardi gras *means 'fat Tuesday'.*
- *It is the last big celebration before the* **fast** *of Lent begins, leading up to Easter.*

A painting by Pierre Renoir from 1876.
- *The painting shows a scene in Montmartre in Paris.*
- *Renoir was a leading Impressionist painter who used strong brush strokes and bold use of colour to paint everyday scenes.*

The exciting design of the Georges Pompidou Art Centre, which opened in 1977, still surprises first-time visitors to Paris. The building looks like a giant meccano construction with caterpillar-like escalators attached to the outside and huge colourful pipes and tubes standing high above the street.

Painters and sculptors

Some of the world's oldest paintings are in France. These are cave paintings in the caves at Lascaux [lass-koh] in the Dordogne [dor-DON-yuh] district of Aquitaine. The paintings could be 30,000 years old. People are not allowed to visit the paintings in case they are ruined by light and moisture. Reproductions can be seen at the nearby town of Montignac.

French people are proud of their famous artists, such as the painter Matisse and the sculptor Rodin. The Louvre art gallery in Paris is where some of the world's most famous paintings can be seen. Leonardo da Vinci's *Mona Lisa* and paintings by French artists such as Ingres and Monet are some of the best known.

Famous French musicians and composers include Debussy and Ravel. Famous French authors of novels, plays and poetry include Molière, Victor Hugo and, in this century, Jean-Paul Sartre.

FRANCE FACTFILE

Area 543,965 square kilometres
Highest point Mont Blanc 4807 m

Climate

	January temp.	July temp.	Total annual rainfall
Paris	3°C	19°C	585 mm

Population 57.8 million
Population density 105 people per square kilometre

Life expectancy
Female 82
Male   74

Capital city Paris

Population of the main cities (in millions)
Paris	9.3
Lyons	1.3
Marseilles	1.1
Lille	1.0
Bordeaux	0.7
Toulouse	0.6
Nantes	0.5
Nice	0.5
Grenoble	0.4
Toulon	0.4

Land use
Farming	35%
Forest	27%
Grass	20%
Other	18%

Employment
Services	65%
Industry	29%
Farming	6%

Main imports
Machinery and transport equipment
Manufactured goods
Chemicals
Mineral fuels
Food

Main exports
Machinery and transport equipment
Manufactured goods
Chemicals
Food and drinks
Textiles

Language
French	87%
Basque	7%
Provençal	3%
German	2%
Breton	1%

Religions
Roman Catholic	76%
Other Christian	4%
Muslim	3%
Other and non-religious	17%

Money
The franc (1 franc = 100 centimes)

Wealth $22,490
(The total value of what is produced
by the country in one year, divided by
its population and converted into
US dollars).

GLOSSARY

advanced technology modern equipment such as electronics and computers

arable type of farming that involves ploughing the land to grow crops

aristocracy the nobility or highest class in society

Autoroutes motorways in France

basin a large area of lowland surrounded by higher land

capital city the city where a country has its government

combine harvesters machines used to harvest crops

deciduous trees trees that shed their leaves at the end of the growing season

domestic flights flights within a country's borders

exports goods sent out of a country to be sold to other countries

fast avoiding some or all kinds of food and drink, often for religious reasons

freight goods transported in containers

glacier a very slow moving river of ice found on high mountains or near the North and South Poles

hypermarket the largest type of supermarket

Industrial Revolution the time when machines were invented which could do a lot of the work previously done by people

International flights flights between countries

lava a stream of molten rocks coming out of the earth's surface

manufactured the making of goods, especially in a factory

Middle Ages period of European history between the fall of the Roman Empire in the 5th century and the Renaissance in the 15th

navigable suitable for boats

peninsula a long area of land that is surrounded on three sides by the sea

plateau a flat-topped upland area surrounded by steep slopes

population the number of people in a country

processed to make a product from a raw material

puys spine-shaped hills of volcanic rock

republic a country ruled by government without a king or queen

Roman Empire the area once ruled by the Romans

Routes Nationales a type of main road in France

suburbs mainly housing areas on the outskirts of a town or city

tax charges made by the state to pay for the goods and services it provides

theme park a recreation area with adventure rides and activities based on a particular idea

toll a charge made to travel on a road

tributaries small rivers that join larger rivers

vines the bush on which grapes grow

waterways rivers and canals used by boats

INDEX